Julius Caesar:
A Reader's Guide to the William Shakespeare Play

ROBERT CRAYOLA

Copyright © 2015 Robert Crayola

All rights reserved.

ISBN: 1511604514
ISBN-13: 978-1511604512

CONTENTS

INTRODUCTION	1
THE ELEMENTS OF LITERATURE	4
MAJOR CHARACTERS	8
SCENE SUMMARIES & COMMENTARY	11
CRITICAL QUESTIONS & ESSAY TOPICS	28
CONCLUSION	32

INTRODUCTION

William Shakespeare's *Julius Caesar* is one of his most famous and frequently performed plays. It tells the story of a group of conspirators who execute a powerful man, and how that decision finally ruins their own lives. Within this framework of deceit and power plays, there is also a story about friendship and loyalty. We'll see how Shakespeare is able to include such opposing narratives in one story.

This guide is designed to make *Julius Caesar* accessible. It presents the play in a clearly structured way so you can quickly figure out what is happening. There is a guide to the characters and a resource for essay topics and critical thinking questions. We'll also examine the various interpretations that have been applied to *Julius Caesar*.

To begin our study of this play, let's take a brief look at its author, William Shakespeare.

AUTHOR: The information we have about Shakespeare's life comes from historical records, a limited range of comments from his contemporaries, and a few portraits supposedly of the man. There are significant gaps in our information, and this has led to a great deal of speculation.

We believe he was born around April 23, 1564 in Stratford-upon-Avon, a town about 100 miles northwest of London, England. We know he died on April 23, 1616, so we assign his birth date to the same day for convenience (we only know his baptism was on April 26). His father was involved in local government and his mother was the daughter of a local landowner. Shakespeare had many siblings. He was the third of eight children and the oldest surviving son. He probably attended a local free school where he acquired a classical education. This would have provided him with a knowledge of Latin, classical literature, rhetoric, and poetry, all of which he uses in his works.

Shakespeare married at 18 to Anne Hathaway, who was 26 at the time. Their daughter Susanna was born six months later, suggesting that their marriage was precipitated by Hathaway's pregnancy. They would have twins two years later, Hamnet and Judith, but Hamnet would die at age 11 (we do not know the cause of his death).

We know virtually nothing about Shakespeare from 1585 to 1592 and what led him to the theater world of London. Some sources indicate he may have taught at a school at this time, but this remains uncertain. The next significant signposts we have are the first indications of his authorship. He had gone to London and was known well enough for his works to receive criticism. His writing career would lead to approximately 38 plays (some are collaborations and some have uncertain authorship), the sonnets, and various other poems. He began a partnership with the play group The Lord Chamberlain's Men (later called the King's Men) at the Globe Theatre, and this led to his financial success.

Publication of Shakespeare's plays began as early as

1594. A collection of most of his plays (called the Folio edition) appeared in 1623. From these works and the plays themselves, Shakespeare earned a reputation as the most renowned playwright of his time, an opinion that has carried on to this day. His exploration of comedy, tragedy, history, and other genres show his versatility.

He appears to have retired around 1613, returning to Stratford-upon-Avon, and dying three years later.

Although the facts we do have about Shakespeare's life are limited, they provide a context for understanding his work, which we will now begin to examine.

PUBLICATION HISTORY: *Julius Caesar* was first published in the Folio edition of Shakespeare's works in 1623. A diary entry by Thomas Platter the Younger (a Swiss tourist visiting London) indicates that he saw a performance of the play in 1599, suggesting that it was written about this time.

THE HISTORICAL JULIUS CAESAR: The events in the play are based on the real historical figures of Julius Caesar (100 BC – 44 BC), Brutus, and other famous Romans. The events take place in 44 BC. Shakespeare knew of these people through the writings of Plutarch, a Greek historian (AD 46 – AD 120).

The real-life Julius Caesar was a powerful figure in Roman politics. He rose to power in the army, was later elected as consul (a government position), and through military conquests that greatly expanded the Roman Empire he grew increasingly powerful. His role as dictator was not universally greeted, as Shakespeare's play shows. It begins at the end of Caesar's life and accelerates events for the sake of drama.

THE ELEMENTS OF LITERATURE

STRUCTURE: *Julius Caesar* as it is commonly published is divided into five acts.
SETTING: The play primarily takes place in and around Rome at approximately 44 BC.
TONE: Tone is how a story "feels." The tone of *Julius Caesar* is full of suspense as the conspirators prepare to murder Caesar. They must act in secret, and there are strange supernatural omens that foreshadow Caesar's death. After his murder, the tone becomes more stressful and militaristic. The final scenes of the play are fast-faced and tense, ending on a somber note.
PLOT: The plot is the play's story. Here is a quick snapshot of the plot. We'll take a deeper look in the summary section:
Julius Caesar is at the height of his power. He has secured a series of military victories that have made him seem like a god to the Roman people. But some of his friends and fellow politicians are not happy he has so much power. Initiated by Cassius, the men plan to murder Caesar on the ides of March (the 15th). Caesar's

close friend Brutus joins their conspiracy.

The day arrives, preceded by many strange omens. The group successfully murders Caesar in the capitol building in Rome. Chaos seems to erupt in the city. Brutus speaks to the crowd to assure them of the benign motivation behind the murder: He and the other murderers did not want to be ruled by a tyrant. The crowd accepts this explanation. Then Marc Antony, Caesar's close friend (and not one of the conspirators), speaks to the crowd. He enrages them, reminding them what a hero Caesar was. They are incensed and begin to hunt down the conspirators for their crime.

Joined by Caesar's nephew Octavius, Marc Antony aggressively pursues the conspirators with soldiers. Brutus and Cassius have their own soldiers, and the groups fight at Philippi. After a violent struggle, both Cassius and Brutus accept that their cause is lost and commit suicide. Octavius and Marc Antony retain power and will continue to rule.

That is an extremely shortened version of the story, but it gives you a general idea of where it is going. It also leaves out *why* these events happen. We'll look at a more detailed version of the story soon.

PROTAGONIST: The protagonist is the main character or characters that we most sympathize with. Despite the play's title, the protagonists are actually Brutus and Cassius (especially Brutus), the key conspirators. Caesar himself is only present for half the play, and he isn't portrayed with the depth and nuance of Brutus.

ANTAGONIST: The antagonist opposes the protagonist. The antagonist can be a person, a group of people, or forces in conflict with the protagonist. The antagonists of Brutus and Cassius are Marc Antony,

Caesar's close friend, and Octavius, Julius Caesar's nephew.

CONFLICT: Conflict is the struggle faced by the characters. Brutus struggles in the early scenes of the play to reconcile his friendship with Caesar with his loyalty to Rome. This is an internal conflict. Once he commits to the murder with Cassius and the other conspirators, the remainder of the play shows the conflict that follows as Rome turns against him.

CLIMAX: The climax is the moment of greatest tension in the story. This moment comes in the battle at the end of the play. Brutus realizes he will soon be caught, and he chooses suicide instead of surrender.

RESOLUTION: The resolution is how the story concludes after the climax has passed. After Brutus is dead, he is found by Marc Antony and Octavius, who will give him an honorable Roman funeral.

THEMES: Themes are what the author chooses to illustrate through the narrative. Here are some of the main themes in *Julius Caesar*:

Succession of Leadership – A recurring theme in Shakespeare plays is the criticism of rule by power and succession. Caesar has gained his authority through a series of power plays and military victories. Following his death, Rome struggles to determine who will rule. In a sense, Shakespeare is using rising Enlightenment values to show the sloppiness of succession in Rome, as well as in his own time.

Fate and Free Will – Similar to Shakespeare's *Macbeth*, there are ominous predictions in *Julius Caesar*. Can the characters prevent these events from occurring? Or is the knowledge of these predictions what *allows* them to occur? In most instances in Shakespeare, fate cannot be avoided.

Ambition – Ambition is what drives most of the conspirators in *Julius Caesar*. Their greed for power is the main motivation in killing Caesar. Brutus is the notable exception to this.

Conspiracy – The nature and functioning of conspiracy is a key theme in the play. We can witness how it grows from a small thought to a full-blown murder, as well as its aftermath.

Rhetoric and Mob Rule – *Julius Caesar* shows repeatedly how people are influenced by powerful language. Whether it's Caesar being influenced by Decius, or Marc Antony swaying an entire Roman crowd, rhetoric can dramatically shift the tide of events.

MAJOR CHARACTERS

JULIUS CAESAR – Caesar is a great politician and military leader. He has recently returned to Rome after key military victories that have elevated him in the eyes of the Roman people. Although keenly observant of others, Caesar is sometimes influenced by flattery and superstitious fears. He is revered nearly as a god by the Roman people.

BRUTUS – Brutus is a close friend of Caesar and a powerful political figure in his own right. He has a genuine love of the Roman republic. He joins the conspirators not out of envy of Caesar, but to prevent a dictatorship under Caesar. Brutus is the central figure in the play.

CASSIUS – Among the conspirators, Cassius plays the largest role in initiating the conspiracy. He is a shrewd judge of character, very intelligent, and good at using his influence to sway others. After Caesar's murder, he and Brutus will form a military force opposed to Marc Antony and Octavius.

MARC ANTONY – Antony is a close friend of Caesar, not included in the conspiracy to kill him. Antony will speak at Caesar's funeral and incite the

Roman people to oppose the conspirators. Later, he will join Octavius and battle Brutus and Cassius.

OCTAVIUS – The nephew of Julius Caesar, Octavius is a young man who unites with Antony and Lepidus to rule Rome. He plays a key role in battling the conspirators.

PORTIA – Portia is Brutus's wife. She is intelligent and can tell that Brutus is planning something with the other men, but he hasn't told her his plans. She confronts him about his strange behavior. He promises to tell her what is going on.

CALPURNIA – Calpurnia is Julius Caesar's wife. She has had strange dreams about Caesar's death. She begs him not to go to the capitol on the ides of March, but he ignores her pleas and goes anyway.

CASCA – Casca is a government official. He is cautious and slow to reveal his feelings about Caesar toward Cassius. He finally joins the conspirators, and he is the first person to stab Caesar.

FLAVIUS AND MURELLUS – Flavius and Murellus are two tribunes who begin the play. They criticize the common people for giving Caesar god-like status. They are punished for removing decorations from the statues of Caesar.

CICERO – Cicero is an older politician, largely regarded as one of Rome's great orators. The conspirators decide not to include him in the conspiracy.

LEPIDUS – After Caesar's death, a triumvirate (rule by three people) is formed between Octavius, Marc Antony, and Lepidus. Lepidus is largely subservient to the other two men, and they look down upon him.

DECIUS – Decius is another conspirator. He visits Caesar on the morning of the murder and convinces Caesar that Calpurnia's dreams are not dangerous omens.

SCENE SUMMARIES & COMMENTARY

ACT 1

ACT 1, SCENE 1: As with many Shakespeare plays, *Julius Caesar* begins not with the main characters, but with very minor characters. This allows Shakespeare to reflect on the main characters from a distance. Since the political figures of *Julius Caesar* are some of the most famous people in Rome, Shakespeare shows how they appear to the common man on the street.

Two tribunes (representatives of the people) walk through the streets of Rome. They are Flavius and Murellus. They come upon a group of men who appear to be celebrating something. The tribunes ask them why they aren't working today, and one man (a "cobbler," or man who repairs shoes) answers the tribunes in a humorous and disrespectful way. The men finally reveal that they are celebrating Julius Caesar's political victory over Pompey (another powerful man in Roman politics) and his sons. The tribunes are angry at the men for this. Pompey was once a respected figure in Rome, but he has been quickly forgotten as people idolize Caesar and give him more power.

The tribunes send the men away. Then they go to remove any crowns or ornaments that have been placed upon Caesar's image throughout the city.

This opening scene does more to establish the setting than anything else. We can already see the conflict that is building. The government officials are leery of Caesar and his growing power. Meanwhile, the common man has elevated Caesar to superhuman status. These characters are largely unimportant to the play as a whole. They serve more as a prologue, setting up the atmosphere for the central characters.

ACT 1, SCENE 2: The main characters are introduced in a scene of great fanfare. Large crowds follow them as they are cheered and admired in the streets of Rome. They enter together: Julius Caesar, his wife Calpurnia, his trusted friend Marc Antony, and many other political allies of Caesar. Among this group are Brutus and Cassius, the main characters in the play. Although *Julius Caesar* is the title of the play, he is not the main character. His murder and its aftermath will be central to the story, but that story will focus on Brutus and Cassius. Brutus is highly esteemed by Caesar. Cassius, on the other hand, is mistrusted by Caesar for his "lean and hungry look," for excessive time spent reading, and for his ability to look into the motivations of men.

As Caesar enters with this train of followers, there is a great deal of pomp and ceremony. Caesar asks Marc Antony to touch Calpurnia. Caesar is very superstitious and believes that if his wife is touched by Antony during the feast of the Lupercal (which they are celebrating), it will allow her to bear children.

They are interrupted by a man in the street. He shouts a warning to Caesar to beware the "Ides of March" (March 15th). The man is a soothsayer, a fortune teller. Caesar disregards the warning and they exit the stage for a time.

Brutus and Cassius remain on stage to speak alone. They both lack Marc Antony's spirit when it comes to praising Caesar and giving him honors. In fact, Cassius has already determined that Caesar must not remain in power. He speaks with Brutus to begin persuading him to join his conspiracy. Cassius points out that Caesar is just a man. Cassius has even saved Caesar from drowning. Along with Caesar's epileptic fits, it is obvious to Cassius that Caesar is no better than him. He does not like the way Caesar is gaining power, and he fears he will become a tyrant. Although Brutus agrees with much of what Cassius says, there is still a great deal of hesitation in him. He is not ready to directly oppose Caesar, and Cassius can see this. Cassius is a master of rhetoric and argument, and he knows how to flatter and convince people. He is slowly working his art on Brutus and other men, but he must be cautious. If it is discovered he is opposing Caesar he will certainly be tried for treason.

Caesar and the others return onstage. Caesar voices his suspicions of Cassius to Marc Antony, who assures him that Cassius means him no harm. This will be the first of several times that Caesar allows his intuition to be overruled by others.

As the group leaves the stage once again, Cassius pulls Casca aside. Casca is another powerful political figure who Cassius hopes to add to his conspiracy. He asks Casca what happened with Caesar just a moment before (when the group was offstage). Brutus and Cassius had heard shouting. Casca explains that Marc Antony offered

Caesar a crown three times, and he three times refused, for which the crowd cheered him. Cassius views the common people as a "herd" that is easily swayed. He feels that people would gladly give up their power to a tyrant like Caesar. Casca senses the general tone of Cassius's talk, but he acts largely indifferent. He is not yet ready to openly admit his disdain of Caesar. Cassius invites Casca to dine with him, and they agree to meet tomorrow night. Cassius also plans to talk further with Brutus tomorrow.

When alone, Cassius talks to the audience. He is coordinating the conspiracy, and without him it might never take effect. He can see that Brutus is still on the fence about the matter. To help him make his decision, Cassius decides to throw some letters at Brutus's window that night, seeming to come from common citizens, and praising Brutus for his greatness. In this way, Cassius will flatter Brutus and play upon the ambition that he sees in him. Cassius provides a vision of Brutus with more power in the future, and this will spur him on.

ACT 1, SCENE 2: It is a dark and fearful night with thunder and lightning. Casca and Cicero encounter each other and are initially cautious (Casca has his sword drawn). When they realize who the other person is they relax a little. They recount to each other the strange things they have seen that night, unusual supernatural sights. A lion walked through the capitol, nature seems to be rebelling against itself, and people have a haunted disposition. Cicero bids Casca farewell and leaves.

Cassius then joins Casca. He believes the strange events of that night are signs from the gods that something is awry. He lets Casca draw the conclusion that it is Caesar that is causing these disturbances, and they agree to plot against him. Cassius reveals that he has been working to get other men to join his cause. Cinna, another Roman in the conspiracy, joins them. They talk about Brutus, the most important man they hope to get on their side. Brutus is powerful and highly respected, so it is essential that he joins them. To sway him further, Cassius gives Cinna more letters praising Brutus. They will put them in places that Brutus can discover them.

Shakespeare shows the extent and growing speed of the conspiracy in this scene. Cassius has orchestrated much behind the scenes, and these implications of earlier events help to reveal the character of Cassius, as opposed to the facade he puts on as his public face.

ACT 2

ACT 2, SCENE 1: It's the middle of the night. Brutus is alone in his orchard, thinking about the danger Caesar may or may not pose. He has no personal reason to conspire against him, but he is also aware that people change as they gain more and more power. Who knows what Caesar might become if his ambition goes unchecked?

Brutus's servant Lucius discovers another letter in praise of Brutus and gives it to him. He also learns that today is the 15th of March, and we may recall the soothsayer who warned Caesar to beware the ides of March.

Lucius then informs Brutus that Cassius is there to see him. Other men are with Cassius, but Lucius was unable to see their faces. Brutus invites them in to speak with him. The men are the conspirators. Cassius speaks to Brutus privately and Brutus commits to their cause. The effort Cassius exerted to sway Brutus has paid off.

They discuss the details of murdering Caesar. Most of

the conspirators want to kill Marc Antony too. He is too loyal to Caesar. But Brutus urges moderation so they won't appear too violent, and he says that Antony will be no danger with Caesar gone.

They also consider bringing Cicero, an elderly and wise senator, into the conspiracy. Once again, the voice of Brutus overrules the others and they decide to leave Cicero out of it.

Finally, they agree to visit Caesar that morning and urge him to go to the capitol with them. They worry that he might want to remain home out of fear and superstition.

When the conspirators are gone, Brutus's wife Portia speaks with him. He hasn't told her of the plan to murder Caesar. He tries to convince her that his strange behavior is due to illness, but she knows him better than that. She begs him to treat her like a wife and confide in her. He finally promises to tell her later.

A man named Ligarius comes to speak with Brutus. Ligarius says that something ails him, and he clearly wants to join the conspiracy. Brutus accompanies him offstage to enlist his aid in the murder of Caesar.

This scene shows how quickly the conspiracy is organizing itself. Brutus has taken a central role in planning the murder. We may wonder how much Brutus's own actions are (ironically) guided by ambition. He clearly cares about the Roman republic, but personal flattery may have affected him.

ACT 2, SCENE 2: It is the early hours of the morning now. Julius Caesar is in his home, and the night has been restless. Nature continues to act strange and violent, and nightmarish visions that seem like dreams are reported by Caesar's guards. His wife Calpurnia has also dreamed that Caesar will be murdered. She begs him not to go to the Senate house that day. The augurers (who make predictions about the future) also warn Caesar not to leave home. With so many dark omens, Caesar agrees to stay home.

Then one of the conspirators, Decius Brutus (not to be confused with Brutus), arrives. He hears about Calpurnia's dreams and offers a more benign interpretation: He says that Caesar's blood will revive Rome, and that there is no danger to Caesar himself. This interpretation pleases Caesar. Furthermore, there is a mocking tone in Decius's speech. Caesar refuses to look like a coward. The other conspirators arrive and he agrees to accompany them to the Senate. Marc Antony also joins them, and they drink wine before leaving.

Julius Caesar doesn't have much stage presence in the play. His few scenes depict him as a superstitious and fearful man, easily swayed by the opinions of others. This is a Julius Caesar past his prime, and an easy target for the murderers. It's easy to see the perspective of Brutus and Cassius at this point in the story.

ACT 2, SCENE 3: Artemidorus, a friend of Caesar's, has discovered the plot to murder him. He has written a letter informing Caesar who the conspirators are, and he plans to give him the letter as he passes to the Senate. He reads the letter so we (the audience) may know that he has discovered all of the conspirators by name. If Caesar reads this, the murder may well be prevented and Brutus, Cassius, and the others will lose their lives.

ACT 2, SCENE 4: Brutus's wife Portia is anxious. She senses that something is going to happen that day. She will send Lucius to the Capitol to see if Brutus is well.

The soothsayer passes, the one who earlier warned Caesar to beware the ides of March. Portia remembers him and asks if he knows of any danger to Caesar. He is not certain, but he fears some threat on Caesar's life.

It's interesting how Portia wants to do much in this scene, but she is limited (as she acknowledges) because she is a woman. All she can do at present is send Lucius to check on Brutus and hope for the best. Both her and Calpurnia have a great deal of sense and intuitive wisdom, and it is largely ignored because they are women.

ACT 3

ACT 3, SCENE 1: This scene contains the murder of Julius Caesar, almost exactly in the middle of the play. This means that Julius Caesar will be absent for half of the story, because as we said, he is not the main character. He is almost like an object or device that the other characters respond to, and not a character of depth himself.

The scene begins with Caesar walking with a large group of politicians and friends toward the capitol building. Caesar sees the soothsayer who had warned him to "beware the ides of March," and Caesar points out that the ides of March have arrived and he seems to be fine. The soothsayer cleverly says that the day is not over yet.

Artemidorus tries to give Caesar his letter warning him about the assassins, but he is overzealous in his attempt and Caesar ignores him.

A man named Popillus says to Cassius, "I wish your enterprise today may thrive," and Cassius fears that he plans to warn Caesar, but this is not the case. The conspirators are on edge because it seems like anything might destroy their plans.

They enter the capitol. Marc Antony is led away from

Caesar by Trebonius. They know that Antony can't be there when the murder takes place – he is too close a friend of Caesar. Then the conspirators begin to plea with Caesar about a man named Publius Cimber who had been exiled. They ask that he be allowed to return to Rome. Caesar is surprised by the sudden request, and doubly surprised that Brutus is among those asking for the man's return. As these pleas take place, they stab Caesar. Casca is first to strike, and Brutus is last. When Caesar sees that his friend Brutus is among those killing him he says, "Et tu, Brute?" This means, "And you, Brutus?" He is unable to imagine his friend hurting him like this, and he stops struggling and soon dies.

Immediately they set to work "spinning" the story of how to frame Caesar's death. "Tyranny is dead!" they cry in the streets. Caesar is no longer the hero, but a power-hungry tyrant. They want it to appear that Caesar's death is a victory for Roman liberty.

They cover their hands with Caesar's blood. This might seem cold-hearted to our modern eyes, but it has a ceremonial background in Rome. It signifies their connection to the dead, and the continuation of a lineage.

A servant of Marc Antony approaches the conspirators. Antony has heard about Caesar's death and wants to know their intentions toward him. He naturally expects, as Caesar's closest ally, that they mean him harm. Brutus assures the servant that they mean Marc Antony no harm and that their violence is over. They ask Marc Antony to come speak with them. Cassius is fearful Antony may be a danger to them, but Brutus says they must treat Antony as a friend.

Marc Antony arrives and is greatly grieved to see Caesar's corpse. He still thinks they might kill him in a similar manner. Brutus assures him that he will not be harmed, and that he will come to see they were right to kill Caesar. A careful tactician, Antony agrees to befriend them for now, and asks that he might speak at Caesar's funeral. Cassius is once again cautious and doesn't want to allow it, but once again Brutus overrules him. Antony will be allowed to speak.

The conspirators leave Marc Antony alone with Caesar's corpse. Antony speaks his true mind and we see he is not at all friendly toward the conspirators. He is plotting how to best defeat them.

A servant then enters. He is a messenger of Octavius Caesar, nephew to Julius Caesar. Octavius has a powerful military faction on his side, but Antony tells the messenger to warn him about coming to Rome, that the city's mood is too uncertain at present. The conspirators would see Octavius as a threat and try to kill him too. But already the alliance between Antony and Octavius is being formed. Their military and political alliance will ultimately prove the undoing of Brutus and Cassius. The conspirators managed to kill Caesar as planned, but they are sloppy in handling the aftermath. Whoever can sway the Roman people to their perspective will have the most power, and Marc Antony is a powerful orator, as we shall see in the next scene.

ACT 3, SCENE 2: This scene will show us the response of the Roman public to Caesar's murder. Shakespeare puts a small group of actors together on stage to represent a larger crowd than could possibly fit in a theater.

At first, the crowd is angry at Brutus for killing Caesar. He speaks with a great deal of skill and calms them. Then he makes them see him as a friend of Caesar, but someone who couldn't stand by idly as his friend became overambitious. The people recognize that Caesar's murder was justified. The crowd wants to depart with Brutus, but he asks them to stay and hear Marc Antony's eulogy for Caesar. Brutus leaves alone.

The crowd is initially hostile to Antony. They have decided Caesar really was a tyrant. Antony was Caesar's friend, and they don't want to hear praise for a man they perceive as a villain.

Antony is very careful in his speech. Rather than argue with the crowd, he agrees that the murderers are "honorable men" and that Caesar was ambitious. But he also reminds the Roman people of the greatness Caesar brought to Rome, his military victories, the money he added to the treasury, his compassion for the poor, and how Caesar refused to accept the crown Antony offered him.

Apparently overcome by grief, Antony must pause in his speech. This gives the Romans a chance to confer among themselves. They are an easily swayed group and find themselves sympathizing with Caesar once again. The conspirators now appear to be the true villains.

Marc Antony tells the crowd that he has Caesar's will, but he refuses to read it. Since Caesar was just murdered, why does Antony have his will? This seems very unusual, and we may suppose that the will is a fake, that Antony is just making up its contents to incite the mob. The crowd urges him to read it. It reveals that Caesar has left every Roman citizen a small amount of money, and that Caesar's private land will be converted into parks for the Roman people to enjoy. The crowd had already been in sympathy with Caesar. Now they view him nearly as a god once again.

The Roman mob is furious with the conspirators. They go to seek the men who killed Caesar and exact their revenge on them.

Marc Antony remains behind. He had claimed to be no great speaker, but he clearly is capable of influencing people.

A servant from Octavius comes again. Antony agrees to speak with Octavius now. Also, the messenger tells Antony that Brutus and Cassius have fled Rome. Apparently they received word that Antony had provoked the crowd against them.

The depiction of the Roman crowd in this scene is largely negative. Shakespeare shows people who are little more than sheep, easily led from one extreme to the other.

ACT 3, SCENE 3: A man named Cinna walks the streets of Rome and is confronted by an angry mob. They interrogate him and learn that he's going to Caesar's funeral as a friend, which angers them. What's worse, Cinna has the same name as one of the conspirators, with whom they confuse him. Continuing to show the dangers of a mob mentality, the crowd attacks Cinna and takes him offstage. The mob is so bloodthirsty for conspirators that innocents will suffer as they vent their sloppy rage.

ACT 4

ACT 4, SCENE 1: Some time has passed. Marc Antony, Octavius, and a man named Lepidus are now in charge of Rome. The country has been divided among the three of them, although Antony and Octavius are the real powers, looking down on Lepidus as more of a tool.

The three of them are deciding who shall die as traitors to Rome. The brother of Lepidus must die, and so must Antony's nephew. Whatever tyranny existed under Caesar, there is still a great deal of oppression under this new regime. We can already see that things are tense between Antony and Octavius – and following the events of the play, they eventually became enemies.

ACT 4, SCENE 2: This is a crucial scene in the play. It also presents some puzzles that suggest revision by Shakespeare (or someone else).

Brutus and Cassius are far from Rome. They are meeting after some time apart, and they are both greatly stressed as they struggle to survive and maintain their armies. Armies are expensive, and they're running short on funds.

Brutus learns from his officer Lucillius that he has been greeted fairly coldly (but honorably) by Cassius. Once great friends, Brutus ad Cassius have been driven apart by the stress of civil war. Their struggle against the triumvirate of Octavius, Antony, and Lepidus is not going well.

Cassius and his men arrive. Cassius immediately addresses the conflict that has affected him and Brutus. Brutus urges him to come within his tent to discuss the matter. It would not look good to argue in front of their troops.

When they talk, there is a great deal of accusations, as well as passive aggressive behavior. Brutus suggests that Cassius has taken bribes and looked the other way when a subordinate took bribes. Naturally, Cassius is greatly offended by these accusations. They argue a great deal about money and honesty. It's clear that the stress of the war is driving them apart. It seems like they might even fight each other.

Realizing that they are still friends and love each other, they concede that their tempers got the best of them, and they forgive each other.

Strangely, just as their friendship is renewed, a poet

gets past their guards to speak with them, telling them that they should be friends. This intrusion is inexplicable, and is perhaps part of a larger scene that was changed in revision. The man is quickly taken away.

It is late and Brutus prepares to sleep. He has his servant boy Lucius sing and play upon an instrument, but the boy is also overworked and soon passes out. All seems quiet. Brutus tries to read a little. Without warning, the ghost of Julius Caesar visits him. It tells Brutus that he will see him again at Philippi, where their armies will soon be heading to battle Octavius and Antony. Brutus hardly has time to react to the ghost, and suddenly it is gone.

The emotions of fear and shock that Brutus had stifled suddenly catch up with him. He wakes Lucius and soldiers in his tent. He hopes that one of them might have woken and called out in his sleep, but this does not seem to be the case. The vision of Caesar is a dark omen for Brutus, similar to the prophecies of the witches in Shakespeare's *Macbeth*.

Unable to sleep, Brutus alerts Cassius that they will be marching on as soon as possible.

ACT 5

ACT 5, SCENE 1: At Philippi, Octavius and Antony wait with their army as Brutus and Cassius draw near with their own troops. Antony had told Octavius that they would not attack them there, and Octavius is eager to point out Antony's error. The strife between these two allies is growing and they dispute battle tactics as well.

Before the battle begins, Brutus and Cassius call for a parley – a conversation between them, Octavius, and Antony. They meet and mainly just recall Caesar's murder. Both Antony and Octavius have a lot of anger that they are ready to unleash on the conspirators.

Cassius and Brutus return to their army. They know there is a good chance they may die in battle. "If we do meet again, why, we shall smile," says Brutus. "If not, why then, this parting was well made." They are close friends again, and it's easy to appreciate their camaraderie and loyalty to each other, even if killing Caesar may have been a tactical error.

ACT 5, SCENE 2: The battle has begun. Brutus thinks Octavius's men are fighting without spirit. He sends Messala, a soldier, to give a message to Cassius and his men to begin attacking at once.

ACT 5, SCENE 3: The half of the army led by Cassius is doing poorly in battle. He is on a nearby hill observing the fight with Titinius. Brutus is doing well against Octavius and his troops, but Antony is getting the better of Cassius. Pindarus suggests that Cassius flee.

Observing some troops in the distance, Cassius wants to know if they are his men or Antony's. He sends Titinius to go see. While he is away, Pindarus observes Titinius from a hill and mistakenly thinks he is taken by Antony's troops. Cassius hears this and despairs. He thinks he will soon be captured himself. Giving Pindarus his sword, he asks him to kill him. Cassius points out that it is the same sword that killed Julius Caesar, who is now avenged.

Cassius is now dead, and Titinius strangely reappears. He has not been captured after all. Pindarus was mistaken. He is with Messala, and they lament Cassius and the "hateful error" that has been made.

Brutus and other soldiers enter. They see the corpse of Cassius. Brutus is distraught. He recalls the ghost of Caesar: "O Julius Caesar, thou art mighty yet. Thy spirit walks abroad, and turns our swords in our own proper entrails." The vengeful spirit of Julius Caesar is all too present.

There is little time for mourning. Brutus returns to the field to continue the battle.

ACT 5, SCENE 4: Still fighting, Brutus and other soldiers pass through, while Young Cato and Lucillius remain on stage. They are met by a group of Antony's soldiers. Cato is quickly killed. To deceive the soldiers, Lucillius pretends to be Brutus. The soldiers are glad to have "Brutus" as their prisoner. They rush to tell Antony, but he soon sees that the soldiers have been fooled. Instead of killing Lucillius, Antony praises him and escorts him away as prisoner. Cato's body is also taken away.

ACT 5, STENE 5: Brutus realizes that his cause is lost. Statillius, a man he sent to check the situation in the field, did not return. Brutus believes he was slain, and that the enemy will soon be upon him. He has had further visions of the ghost of Caesar.

Rather than surrender, Brutus chooses suicide. He asks a few of his men to hold a sword so he may throw himself on it, but each one refuses. The group is ready to leave. Most of them go, but Brutus has Strato to stay back with him. He repeats his request for the sword to be held, and Strato agrees. His final words as he dies are: "Caesar, now be still. I killed not thee with half so good a will."

Octavius and Antony arrive to find his body. With them are Lucillius and Messala, men who served under Brutus and who were captured. Strato is assigned to serve Octavius from that point onward.

There is a great deal of praise by all of them for Brutus. According to Marc Antony, Brutus was the only conspirator who killed Caesar for the general good of Rome. He shall have an honorable burial.

This is a typical ending for a Shakespeare tragedy. The mood is dark, and the audience is left to meditate upon the deaths of so many characters.

CRITICAL QUESTIONS & ESSAY TOPICS

These critical questions may be answered in a variety of ways based on your reading of the text. I have provided suggestions in the answers below to get you started, but I encourage you to consider alternative answers as you explore these topics.

1. Why is the play called *Julius Caesar* if Caesar has such a small role in the story?

Although Caesar makes only a few brief appearances in the play, his importance should not be discounted. He can be thought of as a star in which the other characters orbit around like planets. Even when he is dead, his ghost and memory affect the course of the action. So why he might not be the *main* character – that role is clearly assigned to Brutus – Caesar can be said to be the *central* figure in the play.

2. What role do women play in *Julius Caesar*?

Women had little power in the first century BC, even less than in Shakespeare's time. The main women figures in Julius Caesar are Portia and Calpurnia, and their power is largely confined to *influence*, which they use on their husbands. This influence can be vetoed, and we see that when Caesar ignores Calpurnia's plea to stay home on the ides of March. Portia makes a similar plea to Brutus for information about the conspiracy, and it is ambiguous if he actually intends to give her the truth later.

Following the murder, and without Brutus with her, Portia chooses death over an isolated life of uncertainty. For without Brutus, her worldly power and authority disappear.

3. Can Brutus be seen as a heroic figure?

Brutus is very cautious about joining the conspiracy and only does so when Caesar's power seems to threaten the Roman republic and its ideals. His motivations appear altruistic. Perhaps his great mistake is to join with men who don't have his idealism. They are motivated by ambition and greed. Brutus works with these men and cannot be separated from them in the public eye. If his motivations are benign and altruistic, he can be seen as a hero. In this regard, the tragedy of *Julius Caesar* is not Caesar's death, but Brutus's association with dishonorable men. Connecting himself to them ensures his own downfall.

4. What does *Julius Caesar* show about the common people of Rome?

The common people of Rome were known as plebeians. They are only minor characters in the play, but their importance cannot be overlooked. They outnumber the rulers of Rome and ultimately decide who is in power. Shakespeare depicts them in a largely negative light. They are impulsive, shortsighted, and easily swayed by their emotions. When Antony turns the crowd against the conspirators, it is based on his skill at *coercing* an ignorant group of people.

5. Why does the poet intrude upon Cassius and Brutus in Act 4, Scene 2?

The intrusion of this poet between Cassius and Brutus is peculiar. It doesn't make sense, and it doesn't do *anything* to help the narrative. It possibly suggests that this scene was revised, and an incomplete version of the play has come down to us. This could be due to a variety of reasons. Plays were routinely altered over the months and years of a performance, and the version we have may combine different versions of the text.

Along with the intrusion of the poet, there are a few other anomalies in this scene. Lucillius exits and is supposed to return with the other soldiers. He never does, and no one mentions him again. Also, Brutus tells Cassius of his wife's death, but later he tells Messala he has heard nothing of Portia, acting like her death is news to him. It's possible that he is trying to demonstrate a stoical attitude, and most editors leave the scene unaltered. But it's also possible that a revision took place.

6. What role does friendship play in *Julius Caesar*?

Friendship is depicted in different ways throughout the play. The betrayed friendship between Brutus and Caesar stands in stark contrast to the constant friendship of Antony and Caesar. Similarly, Shakespeare emphasizes the lasting friendship of Brutus and Cassius even as their power is being destroyed. Friendship, along with the loyalty and camaraderie that come with it, is depicted as a strong Roman virtue. Note how the play separates weak friendships from true honor and loyalty.

Even between Brutus and his servants is a love that the play clearly highlights.

CONCLUSION

This concludes this guide to Shakespeare's *Julius Caesar*. I hope it has helped you navigate this play and deepened your understanding of all that occurs in its pages.

Printed in Great Britain
by Amazon